P9-CCQ-401

{to}

May this book encourage you
in your decisions
today and for the rest of your life.

{from}

the
CHOICE
is yours

TODAY'S
DECISIONS FOR
THE REST OF
YOUR LIFE

JOHN C.
MAXWELL

NASHVILLE, TENNESSEE

Copyright © 2005 by Maxwell Motivation, Inc.

Published by the J. Countryman® division of the Thomas Nelson Book
Group., Nashville, Tennessee 37214

All rights reserved. No portion of this publication may be reproduced,
stored in a retrieval system or transmitted in any form by any means—
except for brief quotations in printed reviews—without the prior written
permission of the publisher.

J. Countryman® is a trademark of Thomas Nelson, Inc.

All quotations from the Bible are from *The New King James Version*
(NKJV) ©1979, 1980, 1982, 1992, Thomas Nelson, Inc., Publisher.
Used by permission.

All quotations without attribution are assumed to be anonymous.

Design: UDG|DesignWorks; cover, Kirk DouPonce and David Uttley;
        interior, Robin Black

Project Editor: Kathy Baker

ISBN 1 4041 0187 X

Printed and bound in the United States of America

www.thomasnelson.com | www.jcountryman.com

www.injoy.com

Contents

INTRODUCTION

LIFE IS a matter of choices. What will you do for your career? Whom will you marry? Where will you live? How much education will you get? What do you want to do with today? But another choice is much more important than these: *who will you become?*

The only true freedom each of us has in life is the freedom to choose. But once we choose, we become the servant of our choices. Author and professor C. S. Lewis observed, "Every time you make a choice you are turning the central part of you, the part that chooses, into something a little different than what it was before. And taking your life as a whole, with all your innumerable choices, you are slowly turning this central thing either into a heavenly creature or into a hellish creature."

Nobody desires to take the path that leads downward. Each of us aspires to be something more, something bigger. The secret to the uphill path comes in the individual choices we make.

This book offers inspiration and guidance in sixteen key areas that can help you become the person you desire to be. Every day you will be faced with choices in one or more of these important areas. The decisions you make in those moments may seem small at the time. But when added together, they create the course for your life. You can take the high road, the sometimes difficult road that climbs ever upward, the road that forms you into the man or woman of destiny that you desire to become. Or you can take the easy road. You must always make the decision. Never forget: *The choice is yours!*

ATTITUDE is a CHOICE

LIFE IS TEN PERCENT HOW WE MAKE IT;

NINETY PERCENT HOW WE TAKE IT.

ATTITUDE is the Difference Maker

WHAT'S ALL THE FUSS about attitude?
Does it really make a difference? You bet it does!
Never underestimate the power of a positive attitude.
When facing an opponent of equal ability, the right attitude
can give you the edge. Who enjoys everything more, sees
more opportunities, and lives life with greater enthusiasm?
The individual with the best attitude. Truly, attitude is the
difference maker.

As you examine your attitude and decide what to
make it, remember these truths:

1. NO MATTER WHAT, YOUR ATTITUDE IS A CHOICE.
    Circumstances may not be of your choosing, but your
    attitude is all yours.

2. IT'S EASIER TO MAINTAIN THE RIGHT ATTITUDE THAN
    TO REGAIN IT. Fight to develop a positive attitude, and
    then don't let it slip.

3. YOUR ATTITUDE DETERMINES YOUR ACTIONS. Your
    outlook will determine your life's outcomes more than
    any other single factor.

4. **The People You Lead Reflect the Attitude You Possess.** If you have any responsibility for others—as a boss, parent, or volunteer leader—the attitude of your people is a reflection of your own.

Happiness does not depend on outward things, but on the way we see them.

LEO TOLSTOY

Let no feeling of discouragement prey upon you, and in the end you are sure to succeed.

ABRAHAM LINCOLN

PROMISES
with a Payoff

1. **PROMISE:** If you learn from your mistakes and then let them go . . .

   PAYOFF: . . . you will be able to focus on the present.

2. **PROMISE:** If you rise above the pettiness of people and small annoyances . . .

   PAYOFF: . . . you will be able to give your energy to the important things.

3. **PROMISE:** If you take time for physical rest, spiritual reflection, and relaxing recreation . . .

   PAYOFF: . . . you will be able to think clearly and energetically.

4. **PROMISE:** If you enjoy today and all it has to offer . . .

   PAYOFF: . . . you will be better prepared for tomorrow.

5. **PROMISE:** If you express gratitude to God and others through words and actions . . .

   PAYOFF: . . . you will be aware of the value they bring to you.

6. **PROMISE:** If you give more than you receive . . .

   PAYOFF: . . . you will contribute to society, surprise your spouse, and model for your children.

God chooses what we go through.
We choose how we go through it.

The optimist thinks this is the best
of all possible worlds.
The pessimist fears it is true.

ROBERT OPPENHEIMER

Attitude more than age
determines energy.

ROBERT SCHULLER

It's All In Your MIND

HIS NAME IS Roger Crawford. He makes his living as a consultant and public speaker. He's written two books, and travels all across the country working with Fortune 500 companies, national and state associations, and school districts.

Those aren't bad credentials. But if that doesn't impress you, how about this: before becoming a consultant, he was a varsity tennis player for Loyola Marymount University and later became a professional tennis player certified by the United States Professional Tennis Association. Still not impressed? Would you change your opinion if I told you Roger has no hands and only one foot!

Roger Crawford was born with a condition called *ectrodactylism*. When he emerged from his mother's womb, the doctors saw that he had a thumb–like projection extending out of his right forearm, and a thumb and finger growing out of his left forearm. He had no palms. His legs and arms were shortened. And his left leg possessed a shrunken foot with only three toes. (The foot was amputated when he was five.) Roger's parents were told by various medical professionals that he would never be able to walk, probably would not be able to take care of himself, and would never lead a normal life.

After recovering from the shock, Roger's parents were determined to give him the best chance possible for living a normal life. They raised him to feel loved, to be strong, and to develop independence. "You're only as handicapped as you want to be," his father used to tell him. They encouraged him to do everything his heart desired. And they taught him to think positively.

"Something my parents never did was to allow me to feel sorry for myself, or to take advantage of people because of my handicap," observes Roger.[1]

Roger appreciated the encouragement and training he received from his parents, but I don't think he really understood the significance of it or his achievements until he was in college and he interacted with someone who wanted to meet him. After receiving a phone call from a man who had read about his tennis victories, Crawford agreed to meet him at a nearby restaurant. When Roger stood up to shake hands with the man, he discovered that the other guy had hands that were almost identical to his. That got Crawford excited, because he thought he had found someone similar to him but older who could act as his mentor. But after talking with the stranger for a few minutes, he realized he was wrong. Roger says:

Instead, what I found was someone with a bitter, pessimistic attitude who blamed all of life's disappointments and failures on his anatomy.

I soon recognized that our lives and attitudes couldn't have been more different. . . . He had never held a job for long, and he was sure this was because of "discrimination"—certainly not because (as he admitted) he was constantly late, frequently absent, and failed to take any responsibility for his work. His attitude was, "The world owes me," and his problem was that the world disagreed. He was even angry with me because I didn't share his despair.

We kept in touch for several years, until it dawned on me that even if some miracle were suddenly to give him a perfect body, his unhappiness and lack of success wouldn't change. He would still be at the same place in his life.[2]

That man had allowed failure to seize him from the inside.

Chances are that the adversity in your life has been nowhere near as difficult as Roger Crawford's has been. And that's why his story is such an inspiration. Roger maintains, "Handicaps can only disable us if we let them. This is true not only of physical challenges, but of emotional and intellectual ones as well. . . . I believe that real and lasting limitations are created in our minds, not our bodies."[3]

From FAILING FORWARD

Attitudes determine actions.
You are not what you think you are.
What you think, you are.

I don't believe in pessimism.
If something doesn't come up the way
you want, forge ahead.
If you think it's going to rain, it will.

CLINT EASTWOOD

We are either the masters
or the victims of our attitudes.
It's a matter of personal choice—
blessing or curse.

What is an ATTITUDE?

It is the "advance man" of our true selves.

Its roots are inward but its fruit is outward.

It is our best friend or our worst enemy.

It is more honest and more consistent than our words.

It is an outward look based on past experiences.

It is a thing which draws people to us or repels them.

It is never content until it is expressed.

It is the librarian of our past;

It is the speaker of our present;

It is the prophet of our future.

From THE WINNING ATTITUDE

Nothing can stop the man
with the right mental attitude
from achieving his goal;
nothing on earth can help the man
with the wrong mental attitude.

THOMAS JEFFERSON

CHARACTER
IS A CHOICE

A GOOD HEART IS BETTER THAN
ALL THE HEADS IN THE WORLD.

EDWARD BULWER-LYTTON

No man can climb out beyond
the limitations of his own character.

JOHN MORLEY

The measure of a person's
real character is what he would do if he
knew he would never be found out.

THOMAS MACAULAY

Good character is more
to be praised than outstanding talent.
Most talents are to some extent
a gift. Good character, by contrast,
is not given to us. We have to build it
piece by piece—by thought, choice,
courage, and determination.

JOHN LUTHER

What are You
MADE OF?

WHAT ARE YOU made of? Abraham Lincoln said, "Character is like a tree and reputation like its shadow. The shadow is what we think of it; the tree is the real thing."

Do you have a stout heart? Are you strong like a mighty oak tree? Do your roots go deep? Are you a person of substance? When the sky gets dark and the weather gets rough, does your character stand strong like a growing tree, or does it fade away the same way a shadow does when the clouds roll in?

The choice is yours. You can spend the day hoping for the sun to shine, so that you *look* good. Or you cultivate your character, growing it daily inch by inch, until one day it not only provides your strength, but also stands as a symbol of stability to those around you.

When you do the things
you have to do
when you have to do them,
the day will come when you can do
the things you want to do
when you want to do them.

ZIG ZIGLAR

Character cannot be
developed in ease and quiet.
Only through experience of trial
and suffering can the soul
be strengthened, vision cleared,
ambition inspired,
and success achieved.

HELEN KELLER

You never display your character
more clearly than when you
speak about the character of others.

JOHN C. MAXWELL

If I try to use human influence
strategies and tactics of how to get
other people to do what I want,
to work better, to be more motivated,
to like me and each other—while my
character is fundamentally flawed,
marked by duplicity or insincerity—
then, in the long run, I cannot
be successful. My duplicity will breed
distrust, and everything I do—
even using so-called good
human relations techniques—
will be perceived as manipulative.

STEPHEN COVEY

You can't get much done in life
if you only work
on the days when you feel good.

JERRY WEST

A talent is formed in stillness,
a character in the world's torrent.

JOHANN WOLFGANG VON GOETHE

Insight into
CHARACTER

1. Gifts and talents are given to us, but character is developed by us.

2. Our character is crucial because it earns the trust of others.

3. Only good character gives us lasting success with people.

4. Strong character communicates credibility and consistency.

5. Our character colors our perspective.

6. We cannot rise above the limitations of our character.

How an individual plays the game
shows part of his character.
How he loses shows all of it.

Character is the sum total of
all our everyday choices.

MARGARET JENSEN

Some men succeed by what they know;
some by what they do;
and a few by what they are.

ELBERT HUBBARD

How you spend your spare time
is a test of your character.

JOHN C. MAXWELL

What you do may fade away.
What you are survives you in the way
it impacts others.

JOHN C. MAXWELL

Let integrity and uprightness
preserve me, for I wait for You.

KING DAVID OF ISRAEL (PSALM 25:21)

No man can for any considerable time
wear one face to himself
and another to the multitude
without finally getting bewildered
as to which is the true one.

NATHANIEL HAWTHORNE

Sow a Thought, and you reap an Act;

Sow an Act, and you reap a Habit;

Sow a Habit, and you reap a Character;

Sow a Character, and you reap a Destiny.

VALUES
are a CHOICE

TRY NOT TO BECOME MEN OF SUCCESS.

RATHER, BECOME MEN OF VALUE.

ALBERT EINSTEIN

Look at our heroes,
what we spend our money on,
what we watch on TV—
that is what we value.
Changing things is the problem.
It's not a question of hoeing
at the weeds on the surface of society,
but of a real root job.

NICOLS FOX

The real measure of a man's worth
is how much he would be worth
if he lost all his money.

HAROLD J. SMITH

Is it Time for
REALIGNMENT?

YOU HAVE ALREADY MADE choices about your values. Some you might have weighed carefully and acted upon with intentionality. They are likely things you celebrate. Others you have made without any conscious thought and you live them by default. You might not even be aware of these decisions.

How can you discover the unconscious values you've embraced? Look at how you spend your time and money. Psychiatrist M. Scott Peck observed, "When we love something it is of value to us, and when something is of value to us, we spend time with it, time enjoying it, and time taking care of it."

Perhaps it is time to conduct a values audit in your life. Look at your calendar. Review your budget and compare it to your spending habits. Think about your passions. All of those things will lead you invariably to an accounting of your values. If you are living by values that run contrary to your ideals, philosophy, or theology, consider what changes you must make to align who you are, what you believe, and what you do.

Nice guys may appear to finish last,
but usually they are
running in a different race.

KEN BLANCHARD &

NORMAN VINCENT PEALE

There's harmony and inner peace
to be found in following
a moral compass that points
in the same direction,
regardless of fashion or trend.

TED KOPPEL

It's foolish to expect
an empty bag to stand up straight.

Values are like . . .

1. *Anchors* — They hold you steady during rough times.

2. *Friends* — They stay with you and assure you.

3. *The North Star* — They are always dependable to guide you.

4. *A Fresh Wind* — They give you refreshing encouragement.

How to Live Out Your Values with Integrity

1. Articulate your values clearly.

2. Review them daily.

3. Practice them purposefully.

4. Make decisions with them strategically

5 Teach them to your family intentionally.

6. Recognize them in each other publicly.

7. Celebrate them continually.

You don't make decisions because
    they are easy.
You don't make decisions because
    they are cheap.
You don't make decisions because
    they are popular.
You make decisions because
    they are right.

THEODORE HESBURGH

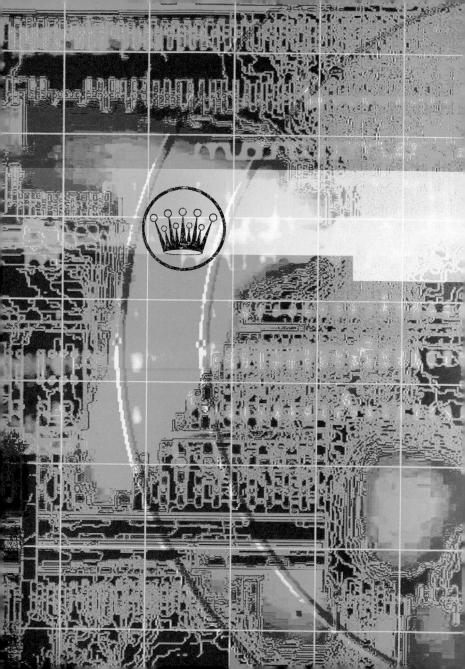

SELF-DISCIPLINE is a CHOICE

IT IS NOT THE MOUNTAINS
WE CONQUER, BUT OURSELVES.

SIR EDMUND HILLARY

What we do on some great occasion
will probably depend on
what we already are; and
what we are will be the result
of previous years of self-discipline.

H. P. LIDDON

If we don't discipline ourselves,
the world will do it for us.

WILLIAM FEATHER

What Made
the DIFFERENCE

IN HIS BOOK *The Life God Blesses,* my friend Gordon MacDonald tells a story about his experiences on the track team at the University of Colorado in the late fifties. In particular, he remembers the difficult workouts he did with a teammate named Bill. "To this day I have anguished memories of our workouts each Monday afternoon," says Gordon. "The memories are onerous because the workouts were. When those Monday workouts ended, I would stagger in exhaustion to the locker room."

But Bill was different. Undoubtedly, those workouts were demanding to him, too. When he was done, he would rest on the grass near the track. But after about twenty minutes, while Gordon showered, Bill would repeat the entire workout!

Bill didn't consider himself to be an exceptional athlete in college. During his years at the University of Colorado, he never earned a medal in national collegiate championship competition, nor was he named an All-American. "I was not a great athlete," observed Bill, "but I had the 'bag of tricks' theory . . . that is, there is no big move you can make in your training or in competition, but there are thousands of little things you can do."[4]

Bill may not have made a great impact during his college years, but his discipline and desire paid off over time. His best events were the long jump and the 400. He kept working on those and added other skills so that he could compete in the decathlon. Through disciplined effort and continual improvement, the unspectacular college athlete who had worked out next to (and ahead of) Gordon MacDonald became a world–famous athlete. Bill was none other than Bill Toomey, the decathlete inducted into the Olympic Hall of Fame in 1984. He set a world record in the decathlon in 1966, won an gold medal in the Tokyo Olympics in 1968, and won five national decathlon championships in a row—an accomplishment that has yet to be matched in his sport.

What elevated Toomey to such high accomplishment was his discipline. Gordon MacDonald's insight says it all: "The difference between the two of us began on Monday afternoons during workouts. He was unafraid of discipline and did the maximum; I was afraid of discipline and did the minimum."[5]

From THE 17 ESSENTIAL QUALITIES OF A TEAM PLAYER

Some people regard discipline
as a chore.
For me, it is a kind of order
that sets me free to fly.

JULIE ANDREWS

No horse gets anywhere
until he is harnessed.
No steam or gas ever drives anything
until it is confined.
No Niagara is ever turned into light
and power until it is tunneled.
No life ever grows great
until it is focused,
dedicated, disciplined.

HARRY EMERSON FOSDICK

Six Keys to
SELF-DISCIPLINE

KEY 1—Train yourself to make good use of your time.

KEY 2—Study yourself, identify your strengths, and
build on them.

KEY 3—Know the priorities of your work.

KEY 4—Give your time to the people who
produce results.

KEY 5—Make decisions quickly with limited information.

KEY 6—Take action whenever possible.

Hold yourself responsible for
a higher standard than anybody
else expects of you.
Never excuse yourself.
Never pity yourself.
Be a hard master to yourself—
and be lenient to everybody else.

HENRY WARD BEECHER

COMMITMENT
is a CHOICE

YOU WILL INVEST YOUR LIFE

IN SOMETHING, OR YOU

WILL THROW IT AWAY ON NOTHING.

HADDON ROBINSON

There is no use whatever
trying to help people
who do not help themselves.
You cannot push anyone
up a ladder unless
he is willing to climb himself.

ANDREW CARNEGIE

First involvement,
then commitment.

You have to pay a price.
You will find that everything
in life exacts a price,
and you will have to decide
whether the price
is worth the prize.

SAM NUNN

I am only one, but I am one.
I cannot do everything, but
I can do something.
And that which I can do,
by the grace of God, I will do.

D. L. MOODY

7 Enemies of COMMITMENT

1. A Lifestyle of Giving Up

2. A Wrong Belief that Life Should Be Easy

3. A Wrong Belief that Success is a Destination

4. An Attitude of Negative Thinking

5. An Acceptance of Other People's Fences

6. An Irrational Fear of Failure

7. A Lack of Vision

One half of knowing what you want
is knowing what you
must give up before you get it.

SIDNEY HOWARD

How Do You Define
COMMITMENT?

IN 1939, a twenty–year–old man from New York City named Jonas Salk completed his training at NYU Medical School. In med school, he began to study immunology, including influenza research. And during his second year of medical school, when he got the chance to spend a year doing research and teaching, he took it.

"At the end of that year," he recalled, "I was told I could, if I wished, switch and get a Ph.D. in biochemistry, but my preference was to stay with medicine. I believe that this is all linked to my original ambition, or desire, which was to be of some help to humankind, so to speak, in a larger sense than just on a one–to–one basis." [6]

In 1947, Salk became the head of the Virus Research Lab at the University of Pittsburgh, where he began investigating the polio virus. In those days, polio was a horrible crippling disease that claimed the lives of thousands of people every year, with children being the most frequent victims. The New York polio epidemic of the summer of 1916 left 27,000 people paralyzed and another 9,000 people dead. After that year, epidemics became common, and every summer hordes of people escaped large cities to try to protect their children.

After more than four years of continuous work, Salk and his team developed a polio vaccine. It's one thing to believe in something you're doing, and another to be totally committed to it. In the summer of 1952, Jonas Salk inoculated healthy volunteers with his vaccine. Included in that group were himself, his wife, and their three sons.

Salk's commitment paid off. The trials of the vaccine were successful, and in 1955 he and his former mentor, Dr. Thomas Francis, arranged to inoculate 4 million children. In 1955, 28,985 cases of polio were reported in the United States. In 1956, that number was cut in half. In 1957, there were only 5,894. Today, thanks to the work of Jonas Salk and subsequent efforts by other scientists such as Albert Sabin, cases of polio in the U.S. are virtually nonexistent.

Jonas Salk dedicated eight years of his life to defeating polio. But his real desire was helping people, which he further demonstrated by never patenting the vaccine he created. In that way, it could be used to help people around the globe. You could say that the team he was most committed to was humankind.

From THE 17 ESSENTIAL QUALITIES OF A TEAM PLAYER

Nothing of worth or weight
can be achieved with half a mind, with a
faint heart, and with a lame endeavor.

ISAAC BARROW

When God measures people,
He checks the heart, not the head.

JOHN C. MAXWELL

If you do what you can,
with what you have, where you are,
then God won't leave you
where you are and
He will increase what you have.

BILL PURVIS

Nobody who ever gave his best
regretted it.

GEORGE HALAS

How to Develop
COMMITMENT

1. Realize it usually begins with a struggle.

2. Understand that it has nothing to do with talent or ability.

3. Recognize that it's not a matter of conditions but of choice.

4. Start with the little things.

5. Settle moral issues before you're confronted.

6. Trust in God

TEACHABILITY
is a CHOICE

THEY KNOW ENOUGH WHO KNOW HOW TO LEARN.

HENRY BROOKS ADAMS

A winner knows
how much he still has to learn,
even when he is considered
an expert by others.
A loser wants to be considered
an expert by others,
before he has learned enough
to know how little he knows.

SYDNEY HARRIS

To be fond of learning
is to be near to knowledge.

TZE-SZE

Make your friends your teachers
and mingle the pleasures
of conversation with
the advantages of instruction.

BALTASAR GRACIAN

Youth is a State of MIND

Empty the coins of your purse
into your mind and
your mind will fill
your purse with coins.

BENJAMIN FRANKLIN

Nothing is interesting
if you're not interested.

HELEN MACINNESS

TEACHABLE
to the End

PRESIDENT THEODORE ROOSEVELT is remembered as an outspoken man of action and proponent of the vigorous life. While in the White House, he was known for regular boxing and judo sessions, vigorous horseback rides, and long, strenuous hikes.

At different times in his life, TR (Roosevelt's nickname) was a cowboy in the Wild West, an explorer and big-game hunter, and a rough-riding cavalry officer in the Spanish-American War. His enthusiasm and stamina seemed boundless. As the vice-presidential candidate in 1900, he gave 673 speeches and traveled 20,000 miles while campaigning for President McKinley. And years after his presidency, while preparing to deliver a speech in Milwaukee, Roosevelt was shot in the chest by a would-be assassin. With a broken rib and a bullet in his chest, Roosevelt insisted on delivering his one-hour speech before allowing himself to be taken to the hospital.

Roosevelt's list of accomplishments is remarkable. Under his leadership, the United States emerged as a world power. He helped the country develop a first-class navy. He built the Panama Canal. He negotiated peace between Russia and Japan, winning a Nobel Peace Prize in the process. And when people questioned TR's leadership—he had become president when McKinley was assassinated—he campaigned and was reelected by the largest majority of any president up to his time.

Ever the man of action, when Roosevelt completed his term as president in 1909, he immediately traveled to Africa where he led a scientific expedition sponsored by the Smithsonian Institution. And in 1913 he co-led a group to explore the uncharted River of Doubt in Brazil. It was a great learning adventure he said he could not pass up. "It was my last chance to be a boy," he later admitted. He was fifty-five years old.

On January 6, 1919, at his home in New York, Theodore Roosevelt died in his sleep. At the time, Vice President Thomas Riley Marshall said, "Death had to take him sleeping, for if Roosevelt had been awake, there would have been a fight." When they removed him from his bed, they found a book under his pillow. Up to the very last, TR was still striving to learn and improve himself.

From THE 21 IRREFUTABLE LAWS OF LEADERSHIP

Live to learn,
and you will really learn to live.

JOHN C. MAXWELL

INITIATIVE is a CHOICE

TO SUCCEED, JUMP AS QUICKLY
AT OPPORTUNITIES
AS YOU DO AT CONCLUSIONS.

BENJAMIN FRANKLIN

Cause something to happen.

PAUL "BEAR" BRYANT

Things may come to those who wait,
but only the things
left by those who hustle.

ABRAHAM LINCOLN

The people who get on in this world
are the people who get up and
look for the circumstances they want,
and if they can't find them,
make them.

GEORGE BERNARD SHAW

"American," in the eyes of the world,
typifies above all else
this quality of initiative.
The great successes are
nearly all the fruit of initiative.

B. C. FORBES

Resolved, never to do anything
which I should be afraid to do
if it were the last hour of my life.

JONATHAN EDWARDS

Yesterday is history.
Tomorrow is a mystery.
And today?
Today is a gift.
That is why they call it
the present.

ELEANOR ROOSEVELT

It's wonderful what we can do
if we're always doing.

GEORGE WASHINGTON

Get Out of Your RUT

SOMETIMES THE GREATEST enemy to initiative is a rut we're created for ourselves. Ruts can prevent us from changing course, even when we know change is vital to our success. Get stuck in a rut long enough, and you'll begin to lose all incentive to initiate positive change. As the saying goes, a grave is nothing more than a rut with both ends filled in.

So how to you get yourself out of a rut? Take these steps:

1. Accept responsibility for your own life.

2. Know where you want to be.

3. Divide your dream into manageable parts.

4. Get going.

Don't hope for inspiration. Create your own incentive to change. Don't wait—create the initiative you need for your success.

The Rewards
of INITIATIVE

THE WORLD BESTOWS its prizes, both its money and honors, on one thing and that's initiative. What is initiative? I will tell you. It is doing the right thing without being told. But next to doing the thing without being told, is doing it when you have been told once. . . . Those who can carry a message get high honors, but their pay is not always in proportion. Next there are those who never do a thing until they are told twice. Such get no honors and small thanks. Next there are those who do the right thing only when an executive kicks them from behind, and these get indifference instead of honors, and a pittance for their pay. This kind spends most of its time polishing the bench with a hard luck story. Then still lower down the scale than this we have the dullard who will not do the right thing even when someone goes along to show him how and stays to see he does it. He is always out of a job and receives the contempt he deserves unless he happens to have a rich Pa, in which case destiny patiently awaits around the corner with an [iron] club. To which class do you belong?

ELBERT HUBBARD

PASSION
is a CHOICE

SUCCESS IS NOT THE RESULT OF

SPONTANEOUS COMBUSTION.

YOU MUST FIRST SET YOURSELF ON FIRE.

REGGIE LEACH

When the heart is afire,
some sparks will fly out of the mouth.

THOMAS FULLER

If you love what you do,
you will never
work another day in your life.

CONFUCIOUS

Vision does not ignite growth,
passion does.
Passion fuels vision and
vision is the focus
of the power of passion.
Leaders who are
passionate about their call
create vision.

KEN HEMPHILL

The Power of PASSION

1. Passion is the first step to achievement.

2. Passion increases willpower.

3. Passion changes lives.

4. Passion changes me.

5. Passion makes impossibilities possible.

Find your passion and follow it.
That is all the career advice
you will ever need.

JOHN C. MAXWELL

The first thing is to love your sport.
Never do it to please someone else.
It has to be yours.

PEGGY FLEMING

There are many things that
will catch my eye,
but there are only a few
that catch my heart. . . .
It is those I consider to pursue.

TIM REDMOND

I am convinced that
my life belongs to the whole community;
and as long as I live,
it is my privilege to do for it
whatever I can,
for the harder I work the more I live.
I rejoice in life for its own sake.
Life is no brief candle to me.
It is a sort of splendid torch
which I got hold of for a moment,
and I want to make it burn as brightly
as possible before turning
it over to future generations.

GEORGE BERNARD SHAW

Man is so made
that whenever anything fires his soul,
impossibilities vanish.

JEAN DE LA FONTAINE

It is the greatest shot of adrenaline
to be doing what
you've wanted to do so badly.
You almost feel like you could fly
without the plane.

CHARLES LINDBERGH

You will be remembered in life
only for your passions.

JOHN C. MAXWELL

A Fire that
NEVER GOES OUT

HAVE YOU EVER NOTICED the difference passion makes? How many dispassionate successes have you met? How many high achievers *lack* enthusiasm? How many great leaders do you admire who were indifferent?

Passion opens the door for achievement. When you're passionate about what you are doing, commitment naturally follows. You don't have to try to produce perseverance—it sweeps over you like an ocean wave.

Passion turns your have–to's into want–to's. It creates a fire of motivation that never goes out.

People with passion enjoy the climb as much as they enjoy reaching the summit.

If you have passion, you'll never need a jump start. In fact, you never have to push yourself to start. If anything, you must force yourself to stop. Passion will keep you going when the chips are down, the odds are high, the obstacles are many, and the resources are few.

Find your passion
and wrap your career around it.

DAN BURNS

Beware
of FIRE FIGHTERS

WHEN IT COMES to passion, there are two kinds of people: fire lighters and fire fighters. You need to stay away from the fire fighters. Why?

1. Fire fighters focus on what's wrong with an idea rather than what's right.

2. Fire fighters possess a doubting spirit.

3. Fire fighters work behind the scenes to cause dissension.

4. Fire fighters hate change.

5. Fire fighters love the words "yes, but."

6. Fire fighters keep people with great potential from going to the top.

Put everything you've got
into everything you do.

JOHN C. MAXWELL

COURAGE is a CHOICE

GREATNESS, IN THE LAST
ANALYSIS, IS LARGELY BRAVERY.
COURAGE IS ESCAPING FROM
OLD IDEAS AND OLD STANDARDS AND
RESPECTABLE WAYS OF DOING THINGS.

JAMES HARVEY ROBINSON

It is not because things are difficult
that we do not dare;
it is because we do not dare
that they are difficult.

SENECA

Genius is talent
set on fire by courage.

HENRY VAN DYKE

Courage is resistance to fear,
mastery of fear—
not absence of fear.

MARK TWAIN

Everyday TEST

WE OFTEN THINK of courage as a quality required only in times of great danger or stress. But courage is an everyday virtue, needed to live a life without regrets. Why do we need courage?

1. We need courage to seek the truth when we know it may be painful.

2. We need courage to change when it's easier to remain comfortable.

3. We need courage to express our convictions when others challenge us.

4. We need courage to overcome obstacles when progress will come no other way.

5. We need courage to learn and grow when it will display our weakness.

6. We need courage to take the high road when others treat us badly.

7. We need courage to lead when being in front makes us an easy target.

Courage is
a special kind of knowledge;
the knowledge of how to fear
what ought to be feared,
and how not to fear
what ought not to be feared.
From this knowledge
comes an inner strength
that subconsciously inspires us
to push on in the face of great difficulty.
What can seem impossible
is often possible, with courage.

DAVID BEN-GURION

Courage is often nothing more
than the power to let go of the familiar.

JOHN C. MAXWELL

Courage is not simply
one of the virtues,
but the form of every virtue
at its testing point.

C. S. LEWIS

One man with courage
is a majority.

THOMAS JEFFERSON

Success is never final.
Failure is never fatal.
It's courage that counts.

WINSTON CHURCHILL

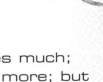

Fortune befriends the bold.

JOHN DRYDEN

He who loses wealth loses much;
he who loses friends loses more; but
he who loses his courage loses all.

MIGUEL DE CERVANTES

There is an agonizing loneliness
that characterizes
the life of the pioneer.

MARTIN LUTHER KING, JR.

RESPONSIBILITY
is a CHOICE

THE PRICE OF GREATNESS IS RESPONSIBILITY.

WINSTON CHURCHILL

The reason people blame things
on previous generations is
that there's only one other choice.

DOUG LARSON

When you do what you can,
God will do what you can't.

Fear not those who argue,
but those who dodge.

MARIE EBNER-ESCHENBACH

Success on any major scale
requires you to accept responsibility. . . .
In the final analysis, the one quality that
all successful people have . . .
is the ability to take responsibility.

MICHAEL KORDA

You cannot escape the
responsibility of tomorrow
by evading it today.

ABRAHAM LINCOLN

Today responsibility
is often meant to denote duty,
something imposed
upon one another from outside.
But responsibility, in its true sense,
is an entirely voluntary act;
it is my response to the needs,
expressed or unexpressed,
of another human being.

ERICH FROMM

Easy Growth
or HARD GROWTH?

DO YOU WANT TO become better? Do you want to grow? To you want to develop experience, maturity, and wisdom? Then make tough decisions and assume responsibility for them.

It's easy to take responsibility for something you know will go well.

It's harder to take responsibility for something that could go wrong.

It's easy to take responsibility when the stakes are low.

It's harder to take responsibility when the stakes are high.

It's easy to take responsibility after a success.

It's harder to take responsibility after failure

Easy decisions can make you look good. Taking responsibility for hard decisions can make you better.

The most important thought
I ever had was that of
my individual responsibility to God.

DANIEL WEBSTER

GROWTH
is a CHOICE

WHATEVER YOU DO TODAY,

DO IT BETTER TOMORROW.

ROBERT SCHULLER

A great secret of success
is to go through life as a man who
never gets used up.

ALBERT SCHWEITZER

I am willing to put myself
through anything; temporary pain or
discomfort means nothing to me
as long as I can see
that the experience
will take me to a new level.
I am interested in the unknown,
and the only path to the unknown is
through breaking barriers,
an often painful process.

DIANA NYAD

You've got to do your own growing,
no matter how tall your grandfather is.

IRISH PROVERB

We are blind until we see
That in the human plan
Nothing is worth the making
If it does not make the man.
Why build these cities glorious
If man unbuilded goes?
In vain we build the world
Unless the builder grows.

EDWIN MARKHAM

Your life begins to change when
you change something you do every day.

JOHN C. MAXWELL

Conflict plus love equals growth.

WESTY EGMONT

You've got to continue to grow,
or you're just like last night's cornbread—
stale and dry.

LORETTA LYNN

The Hot Poker
PRINCIPLE

YEARS AGO, when my friend and mentor Elmer Towns was teaching me about personal growth, he taught me the hot poker principle. He said that if you want to heat up a fireplace poker, you don't put it across the room from the fire. No, you put in right next to the hot coals right into the fire. And the heat transfers.

Elmer said the key to growth is the same for people. To gain "heat" for growth, we need to get close to those who are already hot. Here's how:

1. Spend time with great people.

2. Learn their great ideas through tapes, CDs, and DVDs.

3. Visit great places that will inspire you.

4. Attend great events that will prompt you to pursue change.

5. Read great books.

We are all born ignorant,
but one must work hard
to remain stupid.

BENJAMIN FRANKLIN

Most of us plateau
when we lose the tension between
where we are and
where we ought to be.

JOHN GARDINER

Standards of excellence
are not chiseled in stone.
They are constantly being redefined.
It's important to recognize that
what was graded excellent last year
may not be so this year.
That is why we must
keep mastering new skills.

BOBB BIEHL

Our Age of Anxiety is in great part,
the result of trying to do
today's job with yesterday's tools.

MARSHALL MCLUHAN

If one advances confidently
in the direction of his dreams,
and endeavors to live the life
which he has imagined,
he will meet with a success
unexpected in common hours.
He will pass an invisible boundary;
new, universal, and more liberal laws will
begin to establish themselves around
and within him;
and he will live with the license
of a higher order of beings.

HENRY DAVID THOREAU

Look carefully at the closest
associations in your life,
for that is the direction
you are heading.

KEVIN EIKENBERRY

I don't think much of a man who is
not wiser than he was yesterday.

ABRAHAM LINCOLN

Who Are YOU?

IF YOU ARE TO SUCCEED in your growth, then you need to know where you are starting from. Management expert Ken Blanchard suggests there are four phases of development, each with its own needs. To which class do you belong in the area where you want to grow?

1. *Enthusiastic Beginner*—You need someone to help give direction.

2. *Disillusioned Learner*—You need someone to coach you.

3. *Capable But Cautious*—You need supporters to encourage you.

4. *Self–Reliant Achiever*—You need people to resource your dreams.

Find the people you need to assist you during your current phase of growth. Never forget that those closest to you determine your level of success.

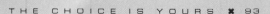

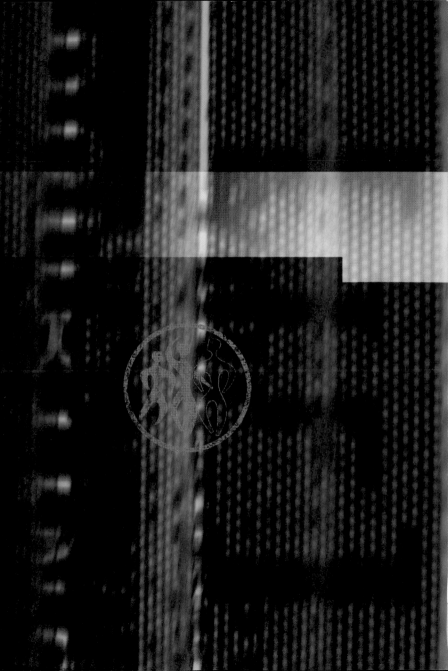

RELATIONSHIPS
are a CHOICE

CARVE YOUR NAME ON HEARTS AND

NOT ON MARBLE.

CHARLES H. SPURGEON

You can give your friendship to others,
but you cannot really ask
for theirs. That is their decision.

JOHN C. MAXWELL

There's no second chance
to make a good first impression.

I will speak ill of no man,
and speak all the good I know
of everybody.

BENJAMIN FRANKLIN

The Compliment Club

IN THE 1920S, physician, consultant, and psychologist
George W. Crane began teaching social psychology at
Northwestern University in Chicago. Though he was new
to teaching, he was an astute student of human nature,
and he believed strongly in making the study of psychology
practical to his students.

One of the first classes he taught consisted of older
evening students. The young men and women worked in
the department stores, offices, and factories of Chicago
by day and were trying to improve themselves by attending
classes at night. After class one evening a young woman
named Lois, who had moved to Chicago from a small town
in Wisconsin to take a civil service job, confided in Crane
that she felt isolated and lonely. "I don't know anybody,
except a few girls at the office," she lamented. "At night I
go to my room and write letters home. The only thing that
keeps me living from day to day is the hope of receiving a
letter from my friends in Wisconsin."

It was largely in response to Lois's problem that Crane
came up with what he called the Compliment Club, which
he announced to his class the following week. It was to be
the first of several practical assignments he would give
them that term.

"You are to use your psychology every day either at home or at work or on the streetcars and buses," Crane told them. "For the first month, your written assignment will be the Compliment Club. Every day you are to pay an honest compliment to each of three different persons. You can increase that number if you wish, but to qualify for a class grade, you must have complimented at least three people every day for thirty days . . .

"Then, at the end of the thirty–day experiment, I want you to write a theme or paper on your experiences," he continued. "Include the changes you have noted in the people around you, as well as your own altered outlook on life."[7]

Some of Crane's students resisted this assignment. Some complained that they wouldn't know what to say. Others were afraid of being rejected. And a few thought it would be dishonest to compliment someone they didn't like. "Suppose you meet somebody you dislike?" one man asked. "Wouldn't it be insincere to praise your enemy?"

"No, it is not insincerity when you compliment your enemy," Crane responded, "for the compliment is an honest statement of praise for some objective trait or merit that deserves commendation. You will find that nobody is entirely devoid of merit or virtue . . . Your praise may buoy up the morale of lonely souls who are almost ready to give up the struggle to do good deeds.

You never know when your casual compliment may catch a boy or girl, or man or woman, at the critical point when he would otherwise toss in the sponge."[8]

Crane's students discovered that their sincere compliments had a positive impact on the people around them. And the experience made an even greater impact on the students themselves. Lois blossomed into a real people person who lit up a room when she entered it. And another student, who was ready to quit her job as a legal secretary because of an especially difficult boss, began complimenting him, even though at first she did so through clenched teeth. Eventually not only did his surliness toward her change, but so did her exasperation with him. They wound up taking a genuine liking to each other and eventually were married.

George Crane's Compliment Club probably sounds a little bit corny to us today. But the principles behind it are just as sound now as they were in the 1920s. The bottom line is that Crane was teaching what I call the Elevator Principle: we can lift people up or take people down in our relationships. He was trying to teach his students to be proactive. Crane said, "The world is starving for appreciation. It is hungry for compliments. But somebody must start the ball rolling by speaking first and saying a nice thing to his companion."[9]

from WINNING WITH PEOPLE

You can't make the other fellow
feel important in your presence
if you secretly feel
that he is a nobody.

LES GIBLIN

Every man is entitled
to be valued by his best moments.

RALPH WALDO EMERSON

You cannot shake hands
with a clenched fist.

INDIRA GANDHI

Ten Things You Must Know About PEOPLE

1. People are insecure . . . Give them confidence

2. People like to feel special . . . Sincerely compliment them

3. People look for a better tomorrow . . . Show them hope

4. People need to be understood . . . Listen to them

5. People lack direction . . . Navigate for them

6. People are selfish . . . Speak to their needs first

7. People get emotionally low . . . Encourage them

8. People want to be associated with success . . . Help them win

9. People desire meaningful relationships . . . Provide community

10. People seek models to follow . . . Be an example

The man who goes alone
can start the day.
But he who travels with another
must wait until the other is ready.

HENRY DAVID THOREAU

Do you want to know how
to get others to like you?
Like them first!

JOHN C. MAXWELL

My idea of an agreeable person
is a person who agrees with me.

BENJAMIN DISRAELI

The Four Levels
of RELATIONSHIPS

1. *Surface Relationships:* The most common of all relationships are ones that never go below the surface. There is no strong commitment from either person, and there is often a passive approach to one another. Though this type of relationship does not reward a person with great depth, it provides the foundation for all other kinds of relationships.

2. *Structured Relationships:* These types of relationships are built on routine encounters. They may be tied to a specific place or time, or they may be the result of common interest or activities.

3. *Secure Relationships:* When people reach a certain comfort level with each other and begin to share more of themselves with one another, they begin to develop trust. They often desire to spend more time together. It is at this level that friendships are tested.

4. *Solid Relationships:* These are the highest of all relationships. They occur when people share complete trust and confidentiality. That leads to a desire to serve and give to one another, and the forging of long-term relationships.

People are lonely because
they build walls instead of bridges.

JOSEPH F. NEWTON

Remember the names
of the people you meet.
You will make a
great second impression.

JOHN C. MAXWELL

Handle people with gloves,
but issues barefisted.

DAGOBERT D. RUNES

Ninety percent of the art of living
consists of getting on
with people one cannot stand.

SAMUEL GOLDWYN

COMMUNICATION is a CHOICE

BIG PEOPLE MONOPOLIZE THE LISTENING.

SMALL PEOPLE MONOPOLIZE THE TALKING.

DAVID SCHWARTZ

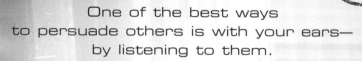

One of the best ways
to persuade others is with your ears—
by listening to them.

DEAN RUSK

Listen to the whispers and
you won't have to hear the screams.

CHEROKEE SAYING

The first duty of love is to listen.

PAUL TILLICH

The ear of the leader must
ring with the voices of the people.

WOODROW WILSON

I remind myself every morning:
Nothing I say this day will
teach me anything.
So if I'm going to learn,
I must do it by listening.

LARRY KING

Leaders Must Be LISTENERS

WE OFTEN THINK of leaders as good communicators. They have the ability to cast vision, inspire, and teach. But as important as it is for leaders to be effective talkers, it's even more important for them to be good listeners. When leaders fail to listen, they create indifference, hostility, and miscommunication among their people.

Leaders who don't listen suffer many breakdowns. Here are a few of the most impacting ones:

1. They fail to gain wisdom.

2. Their people stop communicating with them.

3. They fail to hear what isn't being said.

4. Their failure to listen spreads, creating failure in other areas of their leadership.

If you lead a business, a family, or a group of volunteers, be sure to make listening a priority. If you choose not to, you may find yourself in a lot of trouble.

Genius is the ability to reduce
the complicated to the simple.

C. W. CERAN

The most important thing
in communication is
to hear what isn't being said.

PETER DRUCKER

The greatest gift you can give another
is the purity of your attention.

RICHARD MOSS

Listening, not imitation,
may be the sincerest form of flattery.

JOYCE BROTHERS

Four Communication
STYLES

PEOPLE NATURALLY GRAVITATE to one of four communication styles when relating to other people. See if you recognize yourself in one of these descriptions:

1. *The Retaliation Style*—People who use this style move *against* others. They feel that they have the right to inflict pain on others because they have received pain themselves.

2. *The Domination Style*—People who use this style move *over* others. They force or manipulate others. Dominators destroy the personhood and self–worth of others.

3. *The Isolation Style*—People who use this style move *away from* others. They seek separation, and they never develop a sense of community with others. Isolators destroy any hope of personal development or growth.

4. *The Cooperation Style*—People who use this style move *along with* others. They recognize others' value and contribution, and they seek common ground. Cooperators build trust and add value to themselves and others.

It Starts with YOU

You cannot speak what you do not know.

You cannot share what you do not feel.

You cannot translate what you do not understand.

You cannot transfer what you have not carried.

You cannot give what which you do not possess.

You cannot lead what you have not lived.

Be first what you want to say.

JOHN C. MAXWELL

Real communication happens
when people feel safe.

KEN BLANCHARD

The exact words that you use
are far less important than the energy,
intensity, and conviction
with which you use them.

JULES ROSE

Think like a wise man but communicate
in the language of the people.

WILLIAM BUTLER YEATS

People will accept your idea
much more readily if you tell them
Benjamin Franklin said it first.

COMINS'S LAW

If you want to know what's really going
on in most companies, you talk
to the guy who sweeps the floors.
Nine times out of ten, he knows
more than the president.
So I make a point of knowing
what my floor sweepers know—
even if it means sweeping floors.

KENNETH A. HENDRICKS

The greatest truths are the simplest—
so are the greatest men and women.

JULIUS CHARLES HARE

The void created by the
failure to communicate
is soon filled with poison, drivel,
and misrepresentation.

C. NORTHCOTE PARKINSON

How well we communicate
is determined not by how well
we say things but by
how well we are understood.

ANDREW S. GROVE

The Difference Between a Speaker and a COMMUNICATOR

Communicators . . .

Believe in what they say—*conviction.*

Believe in the people to whom they say it—*expectation.*

Live what they say—*credibility.*

Know when to say it—*timing.*

Know how to say it—*creativity.*

Know why they say it—*application.*

Have fun saying it—*freedom.*

Show it as they say it—*visualization.*

Say it and the people own it—*identification.*

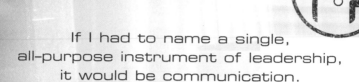

If I had to name a single,
all-purpose instrument of leadership,
it would be communication.

JOHN W. GARDNER

When I'm getting ready to
reason with a man,
I spend one-third of my time
thinking about myself and
what I am going to say—
and two-thirds thinking about him
and what he is going to say.

ABRAHAM LINCOLN

Have an understanding so
you don't have a misunderstanding.

CHARLES BLAIR

People communicate of their feelings and attitudes . . .

7 percent through words,

38 percent through tone of voice, and

55 percent through nonverbal signals

ENCOURAGEMENT
is a CHOICE

ENCOURAGEMENT IS OXYGEN TO THE SOUL.

GEORGE M. ADAMS

Keep away from people
who try to belittle your ambitions.
Small people always do that,
but the really great make you feel that
you, too, can become great.

MARK TRAIN

You can't hold a man down
without staying down with him.

BOOKER T. WASHINGTON

We tend to become
what the most important person
in our life thinks we will become.

How to Become
an ENCOURAGER

1. *Appreciate the Power of Encouragement*—It is oxygen for the soul.

2. *Believe in People*—If you don't believe in people, they won't believe you.

3. *Build Relationships*—The closer you are, the more your encouragement counts.

4. *Walk Your Talk*—Model first what you would encourage others to do.

5. *Show People You Think They're Important*—Remember their names and ask for help.

6. *Give People a Reputation to Uphold*—People rise to our level of expectations.

7. *Reward What You Value*—What gets rewarded gets done.

8. *Hold More Celebrations*—Acknowledging wins motivates people to keep trying.

9. *Encourage Participation and Ownership*—People don't get down on what they're up on.

10. *Raise the Bar*—Many people will stretch to success if challenged.

I'M JUST A PLOWHAND from Arkansas, but I have learned how to hold a team together. How to lift some men up, how to calm down others, until finally they've got one heartbeat together, a team.

There's just three things I'd ever say:

If anything goes bad, I did it.

If anything goes semi–good, then we did it.

If anything goes real good, then you did it.

That's all it takes to get people to win football games for you.

PAUL "BEAR" BRYANT

The secret to encouraging others
is to get excited about the right things.
Some people get excited
about pointing out mistakes
or finding someone's failures.
Instead we should get excited about
their strengths and the
little things they're doing right.

JOHN C. MAXWELL

The best way to cheer yourself up
is to cheer everybody else up.

MARK TWAIN

Flatter me, and I may not believe you.
Criticize me, and I may not like you.
Ignore me, and I may not forgive you.
Encourage me, and I will not forget you.

WILLIAM A. WARD

Why it Pays to Believe in PEOPLE

1. *Most people don't believe in themselves.* In life, it's not what you are that holds you back; it's what you think you're not.

2. *Most people have few, if any, people who believe in them.* When nobody is there to cheer you on every day, you are likely to feel isolated and discouraged.

3. *Most people know when someone believes in them.* Most leaders spend time trying to get others to think highly of them, when instead they should try to get their people to think more highly of themselves.

4. *Most people will do anything within their power to embrace a leader's belief in them.* If others look up to you, then reach down and lift them up; it will change their lives.

I have never seen a man who could
do real work except under
the stimulus of encouragement and
enthusiasm, and the approval
of the people for whom he is working.

CHARLES SCHWAB

Correction does much,
but encouragement does more;
encouragement after censure is as
the sun after a shower.

JOHANN WOLFGANG VON GOETHE

A great manager has a knack
for making ballplayers think they are
better than they think they are.
He forces you to have
a good opinion of yourself.
He lets you know he believes in you.
He makes you get more out of yourself.
And once you learn how good
you really are, you never settle
for playing anything less
than your very best.

REGGIE JACKSON

SERVANTHOOD
is a CHOICE

THE HIGH DESTINY OF THE INDIVIDUAL
IS TO SERVE RATHER THAN TO RULE.

ALBERT EINSTEIN

True heroism is remarkably sober,
very undramatic.
It is not the urge to surpass all others
at whatever cost,
but the urge to serve others
at whatever the cost.

ARTHUR ASHE

Servanthood is the missing link
in most chains of command.

Great people are
always willing to be little.

JOHN C. MAXWELL

A true leader serves. Serves people.
Serves their best interests,
and in so doing will not always be
popular, may not impress.
But because true leaders are motivated
by loving concern rather than
a desire for personal glory,
they are willing to pay the price.

EUGENE B. HABECKER

The purpose of life is not to win.
The purpose of life is to grow and
to share. When you come to look back
on all that you have done in life,
you will get more satisfaction from
the pleasure you have brought
into other people's lives than you will
from the times that
you outdid and defeated them.

HAROLD KUSHNER

Servanthood begins with security.
Only the secure
will stoop down and help others.
And only the secure will stretch and
attempt great undertakings.

JOHN C. MAXWELL

Show me a man who
cannot bother to do little things
and I'll show you a man who
cannot be trusted to do big things.

LAWRENCE D. BELL

The man who keeps busy
helping the man below him won't have
time to envy the man above him.

HENRIETTA MEARS

The Real Man
Behind the BRIDGE

WHEN THE SITUATION is life or death, most people worry more about taking care of themselves than anyone else. Not Philip Toosey. As an officer in the British Army during World War II, he had plenty of opportunities to preserve himself, but instead, he always served his soldiers.

In 1939, he and his unit were called up to active service as war broke out in Europe. He briefly served in France, was evacuated at Dunkirk, and then was subsequently shipped overseas to serve in the Pacific. There he was part of the failed attempts to defend the Malayan Peninsula and Singapore from Japanese aggression. By that time, Toosey had been promoted to lieutenant colonel and was in command of the 135th regiment of the Army's 18th Division. And while he and his men fought well during the campaign, British forces repeatedly were required to retreat until they finally fell all the way back to Singapore.

It was there that Toosey displayed one of his many characteristically unselfish acts. When the British realized that surrender was inevitable, Toosey was ordered to leave his men and ship out so that his expertise as an artillery officer might be used elsewhere. He refused. He later recalled:

> I could not really believe my ears but being a Territorial [rather than a regular army officer] I refused. . . . I pointed out that as a Gunner I had read the Manual of Artillery Training, Volume II, which says quite clearly that in any withdrawal the Commanding Officer leaves last.[10]

He knew the negative effect that abandoning his men would have on their morale, so he stayed with them. Accordingly, when the Allied forces in Singapore surrendered to the Japanese in February 1942, Toosey became a prisoner of war along with his men.

Toosey soon found himself in a POW camp at Tamarkan near a major river called the Kwae Yai. As senior officer, he was in command of the Allied prisoners. His assignment from the Japanese was to build first wooden and then steel and concrete bridges across the river. (The novel and movie *Bridge on the River Kwai* were based on the events that occurred at this camp, but Toosey was nothing like the character Colonel Nicholson in the movie.)

When first confronted by the orders of his Japanese captors, Toosey wanted to refuse. After all, the Hague Convention of 1907, which the Japanese had ratified, prohibited prisoners of war from being forced to do work that would help their enemies in the war effort. But Toosey also knew that refusal would bring reprisals which he described as "immediate, physical, and severe."[11] Biographer Peter N. Davies observed, "Toosey, in fact, quickly realized that he had no real option in this matter and accepted that the vital question was not whether the troops were to perform the tasks laid down, but how many were to die in the process."[12]

Toosey asked the prisoners to cooperate with their captors, but he risked his life daily by standing up for his men and arguing for increased rations, regular working hours, and a day off each week. His diligence paid off, though as he later said, "If you took responsibility as I did, it increased your suffering very considerably."[13] His persistent badgering caused the Japanese to improve conditions for the Allied prisoners, and remarkably only nine prisoners died during the ten months that work was being done on the bridges.

Toosey later commanded a POW camp hospital, where he was known to do everything possible to aid the welfare of his men, including meeting every single group of prisoners who arrived at the camp, even in the dead of night. He worked with the black market in order to obtain medicine, food, and other supplies—even though detection would have meant certain death. He even insisted on taking responsibility for an illegal radio if it were to be found by Japanese guards. And when the war ended, Toosey's first concern was to find the men of his regiment. He traveled 300 miles to be reunited with them.

After he returned to England, Toosey took three weeks' vacation and then returned to his former work with the merchant bank Barings. He never sought glory for his work during the war, nor did he complain about the movie *The Bridge on the River Kwai.* In fact, the only thing in his later life related to the war was his work for the Far East Prisoners of War Federation to help other former POWs. It was another act characteristic of a man who always put servanthood first.

From THE 17 ESSENTIAL QUALITIES
OF A TEAM PLAYER

Self-serving people see
what they have as what they own.
Serving people see
what they have as what's on loan.

JOHN C. MAXWELL

Everyone can be great . . .
because anybody can serve.
You don't have to have a college degree
to serve.
You don't have to
make your subject and your verb agree
to serve.
You only need a heart full of grace.
A soul generated by love.

MARTIN LUTHER KING, JR.

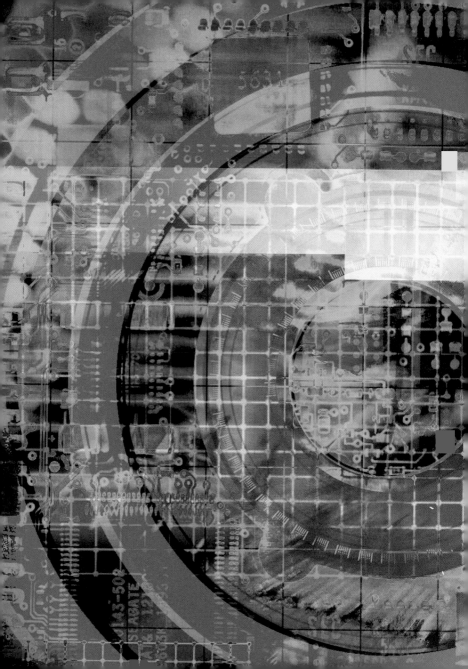

LOVE
is a CHOICE

YOU WILL FIND AS YOU LOOK BACK

UPON YOUR LIFE THAT THE MOMENTS

WHEN YOU HAVE REALLY LIVED,

ARE THE MOMENTS WHEN YOU HAVE

DONE THINGS IN THE SPIRIT OF LOVE.

HENRY DRUMMOND

The love of our neighbor is the only door out of the dungeon of self.

GEORGE MACDONALD

While faith makes all things possible, it is love that makes all things easy.

EVAN H. HOPKINS

The supreme happiness of life is the conviction of being loved for yourself, or, more correctly, in spite of yourself.

VICTOR HUGO

I have found the paradox that if I love until it hurts, then there is no more hurt, but only more love.

MOTHER TERESA

To love at all is to be vulnerable.
Love anything, and your heart
will certainly be wrung and
possibly be broken.
If you want to make sure
of keeping it intact,
you must give your heart to no one,
not even to an animal.
Wrap it carefully round with
hobbies and little luxuries;
avoid all entanglements;
lock it up safe in the casket
or coffin of your selfishness.
But in that casket—
safe, dark, motionless, airless—
it will change. It will not be broken;
it will become unbreakable,
impenetrable, irredeemable. . . .
The only place outside of Heaven
where you can be perfectly safe
from all the dangers . . . of love
is Hell.

C. S. LEWIS

Man of STEEL

AS A BOY IN SCOTLAND, Andrew Carnegie had one ambition: "To get to be a man and kill a king." Clearly, he desired to make an impact on the world. He was energetic, ambitious, and confident. Before he became a grown man, he and his family moved to the Pittsburgh area of the United States, far away from any kings.

Because of his family's financial situation, Carnegie was sent to work at age twelve, and he found work in a cotton mill and in the telegraph industry. He worked hard, he learned, and he advanced. By age twenty–four, he was supervising a division for the Pennsylvania Railroad.

Carnegie would have gone far as a worker and leader, but what really changed his life was something he did in 1856 when he was twenty–one years old. He purchased ten shares of stock in a company called Adams Express. When he received a dividend check for $10, he realized he had discovered the secret to accumulating wealth. He continued investing during the next decade, and his material worth grew. In 1863, he made more than $40,000— quite a large sum in those days. (In comparison, President Abraham Lincoln made only $25,000.)

In 1875, Carnegie opened a steel plant on the outskirts of Pittsburgh and over the years built it into a hugely successful enterprise. In 1901, when J. P. Morgan offered to buy Carnegie's steel operation, Carnegie named his price: $480 million, which Morgan readily accepted. Carnegie's personal share in the sale was more than $200 million.

Carnegie, then sixty–five years old, began to dedicate himself to something that had been stirring in him for over thirty years. He wanted to help others. And he felt the best way to do that was to give his money away. "The man who dies rich," he wrote, "dies disgraced."

For the next eighteen years, Carnegie made it his mission to give—in every worthy way he could imagine. He built nearly 2,000 libraries whose books he made available to the public for free. He founded Carnegie Technical Schools, now Carnegie Mellon University. He funded Carnegie Hall, New York's first large concert hall. He established four museums in Pittsburgh, a commission to honor heroes through the giving of grants, a foundation for the advancement of teaching, and an endowment for international peace.

During his lifetime, he succeeded in giving away 90 percent of his wealth. He came a long way from being the boy who wanted to grow up to kill a king. Instead, he realized that he could make a stronger mark on the world through something greater—love.

Lessons I Have Learned about LOVE

1. *Love People Now:* You never know what's going to happen tomorrow—or if you will see tomorrow at all. Love people now. It's said that the bishop of Uganda, during an especially tumultuous time in his country, said, "If you are going to love someone, do it quickly!" That's advice each of us needs to take to heart.

2. *Love is Vulnerable:* If you love others, then you will be hurt. Because when you open your arms to another, you make yourself an easy target. Do it anyway. Only the pain of never having loved is worse than the pain of having your heart broken.

3. *Love is Powerful:* Love has the power to change the world. It was love that prompted God to create the world. It was love that caused Him to send Jesus to save it. When you love others, anything is possible.

4. *Love Only Lasts with Hard Work:* No friendship lasts for decades without hard work. No marriage survives half a century without both partners fighting to make it work. No relationship thrives without sweat and tears and toil. If you want a relationship to last, you will have to give up other things for it.

5. *Love is Unconditional:* If there are strings attached, then it isn't really love. A person needs to be loved the most when they deserve to be loved the least. When you love people, you keep on loving them. You make their problem, your problem. You stick with them to the end.

You can break God's heart,
but you cannot break God's love.

Things human must be known
to be loved;
things divine must be loved
to be known.

BLAISE PASCAL

Acknowledgements

Grateful acknowledgement is given to the following for permission to reprint material from the published works of John C. Maxwell:

The Winning Attitude, (Nashville: Thomas Nelson, Inc., 1992).

Failing Forward, (Nashville: Thomas Nelson, Inc., 2000).

The 17 Essential Qualities of a Team Player, (Nashville: Thomas Nelson, Inc., 2002).

The 21 Irrefutable Laws of Leadership, (Nashville: Thomas Nelson, Inc., 2002).

Winning with People, (Nashville: Thomas Nelson, Inc., 2005).

Endnotes

1. Roger Crawford and Michael Bowker, *Playing from the Heart: A Portrait in Courage* (Rocklin, California: Prima Publishing, 1997), 28–32.

2. Roger Crawford, *How High Can You Bounce? Turn Setbacks into Comebacks* (New York: Bantam Books, 1998), 8.

3. Roger Crawford and Michael Bowker, *Playing from the Heart,* 12.

4. Christopher Hosford, "30 Years of Progress for the Ultimate 10–Event Man," *Life Extension Magazine,* September 1998, <www.lef.org/magazine>, June 11, 2001.

5. Gordon MacDonald, *The Life God Blesses,* (Nashville: Thomas Nelson Publishers, 1994).

6. Jonas Salk, M.D.: Interview, May 16, 1991, <www.achievement.org>, 2 July 2001.

7. George W. Crane, *Dr. Crane's Radio Talks,* vol. 1 (Mellot, IN: Hopkis Syndicate, Inc., 1948), 7.

8. Ibid., 8-9.

9. Ibid., 16.

10. Peter N. Davies, *The Man Behind the Bridge: Colonel Toosey and the River Kwai,* London: Athlone Press, 1991, P. 56

11. Ibid, p. 107–108.

12. Ibid, p. 99.

13. "A Tale of Two Rivers," *Electronic Recorder,* March 1998, <www.livgrad.co.uk>.